START with
VISION

Presence. Communication. Relationships.
Mindset. Courage. Confidence.

START with VISION

Presence. Communication. Relationships.
Mindset. Courage. Confidence.

LESLIE GROSSMAN

Apricity Publishing ▪ Wiscasset, ME 2024

START WITH VISION

Copyright © 2024 by Leslie Grossman

ISBN: 979-8-9899069-6-3
LCCN: 2024918118

First Edition

"Vision without action is a daydream. Action without vision is a recipe for failure."

— Leslie Grossman

DEDICATION

To girls and women throughout the world

My hope is that you will use the tools in this book to give life to your visions and dreams, and to create a world filled with love, joy, purpose, and peace.

— Leslie Grossman

TABLE OF CONTENTS

INTRODUCTION

It all starts with vision. All of it. If you have
no idea where you are going, where you see
yourself in the coming years, you cannot
use your toolbox of tenets to get there.
Oprah is still one of the strongest examples
of vision clarity. She knew, after a few days
as a talk show host, that she was better
suited to the field of community growth
through sharing experiences, and that
her vision of being a successful journalist,
following in the footsteps of famed
journalist Barbara Walters, involved being
her own version of herself along the way.

I personally have always had a vision. I'm not sure it was labeled as such all those years ago, but it's an outgrowth of my father instilling in me that I could be whatever I wanted to be, and it was up to me to determine what I was going to be. What did I want? Where did I want to end up? What vision did I have for myself?

First, it was to build a million-dollar public relations firm, which I worked toward—twice, actually. With stops along the way on avenues that opened up to me through my circles of collaboration, I did build that successful PR firm. But when I noticed how much my commitment was to women rising in the corporate and entrepreneurial world, I became single-minded. I spent time and effort working for women's growth in business through professional organizations, including my own.

It was then that a coach got me to focus—to sit down and perform the exercises necessary to create a vision around which all efforts would be made. Here is my vision, created and developed over a lifetime of consideration.

My name is Leslie Grossman, and this is my vision: "I am creating a world where gender equality is a given, not a goal."

I have been on a straight course, with ups and downs but with true progress toward my vision. Once I got clear on my vision through my experience and research, including interviews with extremely successful women, I determined that there are seven tenets that each of us needs to embrace in our lives. It begins by identifying the first tenet—vision. Next is learning to incorporate the other six tenets as habits in our lives. Together, they enable each of us to realize our vision and success. Along the way, we each need a circle of collaboration—circles of trusted colleagues, friends, influencers, and experts. This is an extension of the relationship-building tenet, which provides the 360-degree support necessary for our success. The tenets are all key elements in the Executive Women's Leadership program I lead at The George Washington University Center for Excellence in Public Leadership, as well as in my private executive coaching, workshops for women entrepreneurs and executives, and training for professional coaches—all sharing this success strategy with women worldwide.

It takes a village. The village starts here. As you read through the following chapters, think carefully about your own version of how you desire things to look in your own life and where you can apply the tenets. I provide examples of those who have gone before you—some of whom you will recognize, some you might not—but each and every super successful person travels the same route, with different destinations, companions, and passions. Those who lived extraordinary lives have embraced these principles, and they all **START WITH VISION**.

— Leslie Grossman

CHAPTER 1
YOUR VISION

"People get where they want
to go because they know
where they want to go."

— Oprah Winfrey

Oprah was on *The Daily Show with
Trevor Noah* a few years ago. It was an
aha moment for millions tuned in. And it
went viral as everyone stopped dead in
their tracks with Oprah's answer to Trevor
Noah's question. He asked Oprah, as a
person who had interviewed thousands of

successful people, if she found a common characteristic among those who found the promised land.

Oprah shared this insight: *"People get where they want to go because they know where they want to go. Most people don't know where they want to go."*

Do you know where you want to go?

It's called your **VISION**, and it's the first stop on any roadway to success. It might be buried deep in your mind, but it's there.

Why is having a vision so important? Your vision allows you to create strategies and goals to make it a reality. Without a vision, you're meandering through a bog of diversionary explosions and wasted energy heading to a destination unknown.

You might enjoy the journey, but more likely, you will look back and wonder at where you are and how you got there. With a vision, you can plan your journey and make every effort to arrive at your desired destination. On time.

Your vision is an image or idea you have in your mind of yourself, your business, or your life in the future. It's like looking into a crystal ball and seeing your future life in action. It's helpful to have both a short-term vision—one that is just over the horizon (2-3 years)—and a long-term vision—your promised land.

People often get a vision statement confused with a mission statement. Here's the difference.

A vision statement clarifies where you want to go, achieve, or accomplish in the future. It helps keep you focused and on the path to making your vision a reality.

It's a future-focused concept that instantly invokes a picture of the ideal state of the world, a community, or a specific group, after you or your company has made its impact.

A mission statement describes what you or your company will do to reach your vision. It describes your business's intentions and goes some way toward demonstrating how you're working toward making your vision statement a reality.

This is not like what you are going to put on your to-do list. This is the foundation for what you want to achieve. It's going to take a bit of time to get it right for you. It's personal.

PERSONAL VISION QUIZ

To help bring your vision into focus, take time away from your work to relax and let your mind wander as you answer these questions. Spend as much time as you need and marinate for a day after you come up with your answers to make sure they still resonate.

PART 1:

- Why do you do what you do?

- What else would you like to achieve?

- What satisfies you about your current life and accomplishments?

- What are you most passionate about?

- If you could spend eight hours each day doing anything, what would it be?

- Describe the people with whom you'd like to collaborate.

- What results and returns are you presently getting for yourself?

- What are the results of your efforts for others?

- What excites you about what you will do today?

- What, if anything, would you prefer to spend each day doing, rather than what you are doing in the present?

- What excites you about your future?

- Where would you like to see yourself in five years?

PART 2:

After you feel sure-footed in your answers, close your eyes, sit back, and dream for a few moments. Let your mind bring up images of what makes you happy or fulfilled. Consider all the answers to your questions in the self-quiz. This is visioning. You might need to try this a few times, giving it time to percolate. It's important to overcome limited thinking. By opening your mind and creating a vision statement, you're taking the first step toward reaching the career and life's work that fulfills you each day.

You might immediately latch onto your vision. It might come to you in the shower, as you wake up in the morning, or on a walk in the park. Keep a notepad by your bed to jot down your thoughts when they come to you. Give yourself the time and space to let your vision surface. It's a work in progress. And don't make yourself pick things just to cross this off your to-do list. The answers are the cemented foundations toward building the future you wish to attain.

Once you think you have it, then ask yourself the question, "How can I make it bolder? Bigger?" Thinking BIG is part of having a vision. It should not be easy to accomplish.

Still not sure? If your vision isn't clear, here are some steps to get closer to it:

- Review your answers to Part 1 of the quiz.

- Identify common themes and ideas. How do they link together?

- How do they relate to what you are doing now or things you have considered doing?

- Integrate those answers with any images you see during Part 2 of the quiz.

- Write it all down.

- Leave it by your bedside table and review it before sleeping and upon waking. Within a few days, you'll likely have a vision or the start of one for your future.

When you feel you have direction, write it down as a statement in the present tense. Use positive words, as if it already exists, like an affirmation. Always lead with the words "I am..." For example, say, "I am doing such and such," rather than "I am not doing such and such."

Write your vision statement on a small card and keep it by your bed or on your desk. Look at it each night. If it makes you feel good and resonates with you, congratulations! You have your vision statement. And it's fine if it evolves and changes as your vision becomes clearer.

My vision guides me to make decisions about how I spend my time. I always ask myself the question, "If I put time and energy into this, will it contribute to my vision becoming a reality?"

Of course, there are things that I do which will not contribute to my vision, especially in my personal life. However, I make every effort to ensure that the majority of everything I do is either contributing to my vision or opening the door through relationships and work to enable me to live my vision.

Again, here is **MY VISION STATEMENT**:

> " *I am creating a world where gender equality is a given, not a goal.*"

My vision is very different from my mission, which explains what I am doing to make my vision a reality.

My mission statement:

> " *I ignite the confidence and power within women, enabling them to reach their personal visions through my writing, speaking, training, executive coaching, and powerful conversations.*"

Here are some vision statements from those who have been clients or have taken my programs. They are getting close to living their visions in bigger and bigger ways. By writing one's vision statement as an affirmation, one begins to feel it as a reality, bringing us closer to living it and ultimately achieving it.

> " *I am guiding organizations and their people to support each other through hard times for a lasting impact on individual well-being, trust between colleagues, and organizational success.*"
>
> — Katharine Manning, president of Blackbird DC, author, speaker, and university educator

> " *I am creating resilient and healthy communities by working to address the significant global issue of climate change.*"
>
> — Katherine Antos, Undersecretary of Decarbonization, Massachusetts Executive Office of Energy and Environmental Affairs

" *I am creating a multi-million dollar company by impacting the social and emotional well-being of millions of children, teachers, and parents throughout the world.*"

— Bari Koral, founder of mindfulness education company Yogapalooza, training 100,000+ preschool educators; leading YouTubeKids creator; and best-selling children's recording artist

" *I am flipping the typical retirement paradigm on its head by fulfilling the employment needs of the insurance industry with experienced experts who are phasing into retirement but want to remain engaged in work.*"

— Sharon Emek, founder and CEO of WAHVE, now a multimillion-dollar business

" *I am a thought leader in the financial empowerment/literacy space, impacting women and minority communities by eliminating gender and racial wealth gaps.*"

— Michelle Hammonds, Director, Office of Financial Empowerment and Education, Government of the District of Columbia

Corporations have vision statements. While they do differ from personal vision statements, they should share a picture of the future of their organization that may or may not yet exist. Personal vision statements are created for individuals to visualize their purpose and what the results of one's own efforts could look like. A corporate vision statement's purpose is to shed light on the impact a company wants to make and to inspire employees to move positively in that direction as well.

BBC VISION: *"To be the most creative organization in the world."*

The BBC vision is one that would certainly inspire its people to dig deep and be more creative.

> **DISNEY VISION:** *"To make people happy."*

I personally question if this is truly a vision. Disney is a company that has been making people happy for decades. It may be Disney's purpose, but I believe it could be even more powerful. A vision is something that a company or person is reaching for, which inspires people to work or collaborate to achieve it.

> **GOOGLE VISION:** *"To provide access to the world's information in one click."*

Since the world's information continues to change and increase, this vision motivates people to continue to pursue it.

> **IKEA VISION:** *"To create a better everyday life for the many people."*

CHAPTER 2
VISION SUCCESS STORIES

"You can see it everywhere.
Behind every success story
is a vision. In those who
are a mirror of your own
aspirations, determine
what their vision was.
You might be surprised."

— Leslie Grossman

Successful people often attribute their achievements to having a clear vision. At the time they create it, they often have no clear strategy of how to make it a reality, yet ultimately, it becomes reality.

They never lose sight of where they want to go.

MARTHA STEWART

While I have never seen Martha post her vision, here is how I imagine she might have written it based on what she has built.

> " *I am bringing all the tools, techniques, and inspiration of living the stylish and affluent life of the world's 10% to everyone, no matter their income.*"
>
> — Martha's Vision, by Leslie Grossman

Martha Stewart didn't grow up in a wealthy family. As a young wife, she loved entertaining, cooking, and gardening. She envisioned running a popular catering company in her Connecticut town and achieved it. She then expanded her vision to become a cookbook author and television personality. Eventually, through building trusted relationships and becoming a charismatic speaker, she built the Martha Stewart empire, including magazines, products, and a powerful brand. She faced a setback when she went to prison in 2004 for five months after she was found lying about a stock sale. However, that didn't stop her from continuing to live her vision through product development and licensing. She returned stronger and continued to live her vision.

TAYLOR SWIFT

From the time she was a tween, Taylor Swift had a vision to *use her music as a platform for relatable and empowering storytelling*. She was going to use her songwriting and performing skills to accomplish that. She has had ups and downs, but she never wavered from the vision she had cemented decades earlier. Today, Swift is considered one of the world's best-selling music artists with an estimated global sale of 200 million records. Her recent worldwide tour and film made her a billionaire.

STEVEN SPIELBERG

At twelve years old, Steven Spielberg *envisioned being the best filmmaker of the century.* He practiced his Oscar acceptance speech in front of a mirror. Spielberg's vision led him to approach famous actors and directors for mentorship without concern for what they might think of his hubris. Everything he did was about filmmaking. Today, he is widely regarded as one of the greatest film directors of all time and is the most commercially successful director in film history. Perhaps his single-minded approach to his vision is not something that everyone can mirror, but it worked for him and could work for you, too.

SARA BLAKELY

Sara Blakely launched the first product of her company, SPANX, with the invention of a new type of pantyhose that stopped at the ankle, revealing the ankle and foot. Along the road to finding a manufacturer, she noticed that women's undergarments were mostly created by men and were not addressing women's needs. Ever since, SPANX's success has been driven by Sara's focus on her vision: *to elevate women*. She advocates for women through product design, as well as philanthropy for women entrepreneurs. Fast forward 20+ years, and after becoming America's youngest billionaire, Sara sold SPANX and has since invented another new product—called SNEEZ—a shoe brand featuring a high-heeled sneaker for comfort and fashion. She continues to focus on her vision to elevate women, not only in height but by transforming the traditional 'uncomfortable' high heel into a shoe you can wear to catch a train or a toddler and still be on time for the meeting. Brava, Sara!

THASUNDA BROWN DUCKETT

Thasunda Brown Duckett is CEO and President of TIAA, serving 5 million people with investment and insurance services. Thasunda often shares her personal story of her family moving from New York to Texas in a car, which carried her parents, herself, and three siblings along with every possession they owned. Though her parents worked hard, the family rarely had enough food, nor was she able to participate in extracurricular activities with her friends. Her childhood experiences shaped her vision: *to inspire others to save for the future, no matter their finances*. This vision led her to top corporate jobs, ultimately becoming the first African American woman to be CEO of Chase Consumer

Banking. Today, she heads one of the largest financial institutions in the US, TIAA, as the President and CEO. TIAA is the #1 not-for-profit retirement market provider.

FOLLOWING IN THE FOOTSTEPS OF OTHERS

Once you've gotten your vision statement in your mind's eye, explore other people who have succeeded in a vision similar to or mirroring yours. They could be famous or known only to you. Put together a list of those mirroring your vision, and do some homework on them.

- Read what they have written or watch interviews done with them.

- Follow them—their blogs, their social media, their LinkedIn.

- Reach out to them. Tell them why you admire them.

- Set up Google alerts to let you know when they are in the news.

If they can do it, you can do it. If you can see it, you can be it. If you continue to keep it in your mind's eye and in your actions, you will attain it. Now, it could be that NO ONE shares your vision and that your vision is truly unique. If that's the case, go for it anyway. You could be that one person who makes it a reality.

TRY ON YOUR VISION

Spend some time trying on your vision for size. Make sure it fits you.

- What do you look like living your vision? Picture it in your mind. How does it make you feel?

- Run it by a few close friends, mentors, or family members. What do they think? Some will applaud you and be inspired by your vision. Others, including some you know well, may say that you are crazy or that you are thinking unrealistically.

Do not let a negative opinion stop you. People are limited by their own beliefs and often are uncomfortable when others think BIG. People who are willing to visualize what others think is impossible are those who make a difference in the world and in their own world as well. If you are not thinking bigger and bolder than most people, then you aren't flying high enough. Evaluate the feedback; recognize that which you think is valuable, and ignore the rest. No need to try and win anyone over in your quest for greatness. No time to waste. Once you have your vision, it's time to move into action.

A story to give you a
moment of pause.

_____

*The only bird that dares to attack
an eagle is the crow. The crow
sits on the back of the eagle
and bites its neck as the eagle
flies with its prey in its talons.
The eagle does not respond or
fight with the crow; it does not
spend time or energy on the crow.
Instead, it opens its wings and
flies higher. As it flies higher, the
crow can no longer breathe
and it falls away.*

_____

Write your vision out again. Tape it to your mirror and above the bathroom sink or a place you look at daily. Look at it every time you wash your hands and put on your makeup.

- Say it aloud every morning and every evening for a week. And then say it twice each day, morning and night.

After you have completed your vision statement, begin to follow those who have traveled the road before, and you are confident in where you wish to arrive. The following actions must be developed and planned by you to achieve your vision.

CHAPTER 3

SETTING YOUR GOALS TO ACHIEVE YOUR VISION

Once you have clarity on your vision, it's time to set goals to achieve it.

Start by creating a **VISION JOURNAL** where you write and keep track of how you will achieve your vision. List the goals you need to reach to achieve your vision. Under each goal, write out the action steps you will take to achieve each goal.

Take some time to sit quietly and identify three to five or more goals to achieve your Vision. Then put those goals in a comprehensive order. For instance, in my case, when I think back about 12 years ago, when I created my current vision, I realized along the way that I needed to begin with the goal of gaining clarity on why women did not have equality in business or in other fields, like medicine, science, and more.

I already had insights because my most recent business had been producing conferences for women business owners, the Women's Leadership Exchange, for over ten years. We had convened 65 conferences over 10 years, with top speakers and leaders including women's rights activist Gloria Steinem, Dorothy Height, president of NAACP, actress and entrepreneur Jane Fonda, leaders like Valerie Plame, CIA Operative, and women business leaders like Carly Fiorina, former CEO of HP; Helen Greiner, co-founder of iRobot; Sherry Lansing, President of Paramount; Kay Koplovitz, founder/CEO of USA Networks, the first cable television network; and

Sara Blakely, founder of SPANX. They were women who had broken through into leadership positions or started their own businesses, despite tremendous gender bias and discrimination. I had learned how they overcame their self-doubt and barriers, yet I knew I needed to learn more if I were to make my vision a reality. What was holding women back in addition to a workplace dominated by men?

And so my list of **GOALS** and **ACTION STEPS** to achieve those goals began:

GOAL 1

Share my vision with my Circles of Influence.

- Get their feedback, explore where their vision and mine intersected, ask them who they could connect me with in my area of focus; and of course, ask them about their vision, their purpose, and what was important to them so I could support them as well.

GOAL 2

- Do research—books, papers, articles, interviews, etc.—on women's strengths, professional barriers, biases, and how super successful women were able to overcome them.

GOAL 3

- Write and get published about what I learned, i.e., articles, blogs, etc.

GOAL 4

- Do public speaking about what I learned at organizations of all sizes.

GOAL 5

- Get certified as an executive coach and practice coaching actively.

And that was as far as I got initially. Once I set those goals, I moved into action to achieve them.

Upon the advice of my Circle and connections to people I didn't know, I moved forward addressing my goals. Here are some of the results, which I never could have imagined or expected when I originally identified my vision and set my goals. I knew I was passionate about my vision, and it would take time to become a complete reality. Even if it didn't happen in my lifetime, I would work day and night to move it forward as much as I possibly could.

Here's what resulted over the six years by me pursuing my goals relentlessly:

- I created a new website: Leslie Grossman Leadership, which led Wiley & Sons Publishing to contact me about doing a book about networking, which was titled *Link Out* (2013).

- I got certified as an executive coach by Vistage International.

- I was invited to be a senior researcher for the Everest Project (a two-year gig) interviewing C-suite and senior women leaders, their bosses, peers, and direct reports.

- I was invited to work for two executive coaching programs. One was focused on women leaders at a Fortune 500 company where I coached 12 women executives for two years. The other was coaching entrepreneurs who were leading businesses with revenues of over $10 million and were mostly men. The experience I gained taught me more about the differences in how women and men think, behave, and what held women back. Both programs gave me tremendous coaching experience.

- I created training programs and keynotes to deliver to groups of women at several insurance companies, banks, and one New York State college.

- Through an introduction by my friend and executive coach Joan Wangler, I was able to do a 'test' women's leadership program for GWU, which, based on its success, led me to become a faculty director, senior fellow, and launch the Executive Women's Leadership program at The George Washington University Center for Excellence in Public Leadership (which I continue to lead today).

- I launched my own business as an executive coach and business consultant with a focus on women.

- I started a women's leadership training program for executive coaches: Her Circle Leadership.

- And I published my third book that you are reading: *Start with Vision*, published by Apricity Publishing.

Now, none of the above came easily. They all took hard work and many conversations and connections, which you'll learn about under the tenet of Relationships in this book. But I share these accomplishments as an example of how important it is to set goals once you have identified your Vision. Without keeping your focus on specific goals, you can lose your way and interrupt the flow of moving toward your vision. Exciting opportunities will arrive at your door when you voice your vision powerfully to yourself and to others and then proceed on the path to achieve the goals that get you to the promised land—your Vision.

CHAPTER 4

THE TENETS TO ATTAIN YOUR VISION AND ACHIEVE YOUR GOALS

You thought that once you had a vision, the rest came easy? Not so fast. As I said earlier, it can be hard work, but it will be made much easier by using the tenets I teach in workshops and will share here in this book. Consider the tenets your toolbox for achieving your Vision and executing your goals.

PRESENCE. COMMUNICATION. RELATIONSHIPS. MINDSET. COURAGE. CONFIDENCE.

The following chapters lay out the tried and true methodology to approach these tenets. Armed with your vision, the goals to get you there, and these tenets for success, you can be on your way.

CHAPTER 5
PRESENCE

> "What you project in the
> moment has a long-lasting
> influence on those around
> you. Spur-of-the-moment
> responses are for going on a
> picnic because the sun came
> out. Prepare to be present."
>
> — Leslie Grossman

Research reports that within the first seven seconds of meeting someone, we draw conclusions. What is it that elicits a positive presence? According to Harvard professor and author of *Presence*, Amy Cuddy, first and foremost are trustworthiness and warmth. The third characteristic is competence. How can one communicate these at a meeting—both in person or online—in the first seven seconds?

Presence is a powerful thing. It's not just about showing up—it's about how you show up. The way you present yourself can speak volumes before you even say a word. Whether you're heading into a big meeting, stepping onto a stage, or just navigating your daily life, how you carry yourself can make a huge difference in how you're perceived and, ultimately, in what you achieve.

When you're working toward your vision for yourself, whether that's in your career, personal life, or some big dream you've been chasing, your presence can be a game-changer. It's about more than just confidence; it's about being authentic, aware, and intentional in how you engage with the world. People notice when you walk into a room with purpose, when you speak with conviction, and when you genuinely connect with those around you.

Your presence can open doors, build relationships, and create opportunities that might not otherwise come your way. It's like a magnet—when you're fully present, you attract the right people, the right resources, and the right moments to help you move closer to your goals. So, as you work toward your vision, remember that how you present yourself is just as important as the work you're putting in behind the scenes. Embrace your unique presence, and let it propel you forward.

Presence is powerful, yes, but for many women, it doesn't come easily. We've been conditioned by centuries of societal norms to shrink ourselves, to defer, to let others—especially men—take up the space in the room. We've all felt it at one point or another: that moment when you want to speak up but hesitate, doubting if your voice will be heard or respected. Even in today's world, the echoes of those historical forces can still feel very present. But here's the truth—our presence is our power, and it's time to reclaim it.

HOW TO DEVELOP PRESENCE

1. **START BY ACKNOWLEDGING THE STRUGGLE:** Presence, especially in male-dominated spaces, doesn't come naturally to many of us. For years, we've been subtly told to "tone it down" or avoid being "too much." The first step is to recognize this conditioning and decide to break free from it.

ACTIONABLE STEP: Reflect on a time you felt like you needed to shrink to fit in—whether in a meeting, at a networking event, or even in a casual conversation. Then ask yourself: What would it have looked like if I showed up fully, unapologetically? Picture yourself in the same scene. Take a deep, slow breath. Sit up straight with your shoulders back. Take the smirk off your face (if it's there) and transform it into a slight smile. Start there.

2. **CULTIVATE SELF-AWARENESS:**

Presence begins with self-awareness. Know who you are, and don't apologize for it. Your unique voice, style, and approach are your greatest assets.

ACTIONABLE STEP: Take note of how you're feeling when you walk into a room. Are you tense? Overly focused on how others might perceive you? The next time this happens, center yourself. Take a few slow, deep breaths, and remind yourself that you belong here. Say 'hello' to a coworker and ask them how they're doing...with a smile.

3. **OWN YOUR SPACE:** So often, women unconsciously take up as little space as possible—both physically and in conversation. Reclaiming your presence means literally owning the space you're in. Stand tall, uncross your arms, make eye contact, and use your full voice. This isn't about being louder than others; it's about being fully yourself.

ACTIONABLE STEP: Practice standing in front of a mirror or with a friend. Focus on your posture, eye contact, and tone. Take three long, deep breaths, stretch your arms wide and above your head, and embrace the space like a butterfly in transformation. Do you feel timid or more confident? Adjust until you feel powerful and centered.

OVERCOMING SOCIETAL AND HISTORICAL BARRIERS

For generations, women's presence in leadership or decision-making roles was minimized or ignored. The ripple effects of this are still felt today, whether it's being talked over in meetings or being dismissed as too emotional. The key to overcoming this isn't to mimic male leadership styles or to suppress your own instincts; it's to embrace our strengths as women.

Here's the thing: Women bring empathy, intuition, and a unique perspective to the table—qualities that are often undervalued but are absolutely essential in modern leadership. To push past these barriers, we must refuse to internalize the narrative that we're "less than." The more we step into our presence authentically, the more we shift the paradigm.

SOME OTHERS WHO HAVE GONE BEFORE FOR YOU TO CONSIDER:

- **BOZOMA SAINT JOHN:** As the Chief Marketing Officer for Netflix, Bozoma is unapologetically herself—vibrant, bold, and unafraid to be seen. She has often spoken about how challenging it is to show up fully as a Black woman in corporate America, yet she has leaned into her identity, letting her presence make a statement. Bozoma's story is a reminder that presence isn't about conforming—it's about standing out.

- **SARA BLAKELY:** Founder of SPANX, Sara Blakely built her business by showing up as herself. Early in her career, she faced rooms full of men who didn't understand or value her product. Instead of shrinking in those moments, she embraced her unique perspective and leaned into her confidence, ultimately revolutionizing the fashion industry.

FOR YOUR REFLECTION:

1. Where have I felt my presence diminish in the workplace, and how can I reclaim that space?

2. What internalized beliefs about women's roles in leadership do I need to unlearn?

3. How do I want to be seen when I walk into a room, and what steps can I take to embody that vision?

" *How you carry yourself throughout the day is how you define your success."*

— Indra Nooyi, Former CEO of PepsiCo

FUNDAMENTALS OF PRESENCE

1. Small changes in how you hold your body and how you breathe can profoundly impact how you feel. Choose the ones that make you feel more confident.

2. Everyone feels stress from time to time—whether you are about to have a difficult conversation, attend an important meeting, or are negotiating a deal. We each possess the tools of presence within ourselves to step into an uncomfortable situation and address it more powerfully.

3. Becoming aware of your presence in a given moment not only impacts how you feel, but it also impacts what you project to others and how they perceive you

4. Make music your success tool. Your choice of music before a challenging time can work magic on your presence. Your choice of music can energize you, calm you, make you happy, or depress you. Choose wisely.

CHAPTER 6

COMMUNICATION

"I consider communication
one of the things I have
worked hardest on all these
years of my career. I am a
good listener, and I am a good
speaker. It's taken a lifetime
to be able to say that. And,
it was worth every ounce of
effort I have put in."

— Leslie Grossman

At the heart of all communications are conversations. There are two parts to every conversation: speaking and listening. Most people focus on the need to speak well, and while that is clearly an integral part of communication success, do not discount the need to learn to be a good listener. Learning to communicate in a way that captures the interest and trust of the listener—be they employee, manager, peer, friend, customer, collaborator, or influencer—is the be-all and end-all of becoming an excellent communicator. For women, in particular, this can often be particularly challenging due to gender norms in most workplaces. Speaking up, presenting, active listening, trigger phrases, critical conversations, influence, collaboration, and negotiation each call for a separate set of skills, and when you understand which skill is needed in a given moment, you are on your way.

SPEAKING UP

Speaking up is about more than just being heard; it's about communicating your ideas with clarity and confidence, and with a nuance that doesn't turn off the person you are addressing. When you speak up, you contribute to a culture of openness and innovation, showing others that your ideas are valuable. It's crucial to overcome the fear of judgment and focus on the impact your voice can have on the conversation or decision-making process. Oh, and your tone of voice? Practice makes perfect. Who can hear that condescending person, or the shouter, or the laughter when it's not a funny topic?

When others speak up, it's important to give them the space to share their thoughts without interruption or judgment. As a listener, you signal that their ideas are important by giving your full attention and responding thoughtfully. Encouraging others to speak up creates a dynamic where everyone feels valued. Body language. Eye contact. Questions when the moment is right. Repeating back what has been said, so they know they were heard. And perhaps a summary at the end. Or a note a day later acknowledging what was said.

PRESENTATIONS

To present, it's more than just knowledge of your subject; it calls for confidence, structure, and engagement. Presentation training helps speakers refine their message, use body language and presence effectively, and connect with the audience. A well-delivered presentation can inspire, inform, and persuade, leaving a lasting impact. One of the women I mentor and who mentors me, has something she calls the 3 E's: Engage, Entertain, and Educate. Do all three in a presentation, and you have a home run.

Pausing in between important points gives your audience—whether it's one person or 200—the opportunity to take in the message that you've just communicated before making your next point.

As an audience member, being an active listener during presentations means focusing on the content, asking insightful questions, and providing feedback. You can be noticed by the speaker from your place in the audience. Sit front and center. A supportive audience helps the presenter feel more comfortable and confident, improving the overall quality of the communication.

ACTIVE LISTENING IN CONVERSATIONS

Conversation partners are both speakers and listeners. Active listening is paying close attention to what your conversation partner is saying and how they are saying it. When you are listening actively, you are communicating to the speaker that what they have to say matters. It's a two-way interaction that shows you are truly engaged and enables you to 'hear' and understand what they are communicating. When you are the speaker, a great way to begin a conversation is to ask questions about your partner. Listen for any connections or common threads that you share with them. Those threads can lead you to contribute to the conversation and take your turn as the speaker.

In addition to being a clear, focused speaker, active listening is one of the most effective ways to create a trusted connection with a manager, peer, direct report, and even a new friend. When you give the speaker 100% of your attention, without interrupting them or allowing your own head-talk to stop you from listening, your relationship is getting off on the right track.

TRIGGER PHRASES

Words matter.

Understanding the impact of trigger phrases—words or statements that evoke strong emotional responses or convey indecisiveness or lack of confidence—is essential for effective communication. As a speaker, being mindful of these can help you avoid unintended conflict and keep the conversation productive. By carefully choosing your words, you can steer discussions in a positive direction. Beware of triggers that lose the person at hello. How many times has someone not heard your message because of one phrase or word you used in your intro or presentation? Using trigger words/phrases like *"sorry," "just," "I'm no expert," "try/trying"* takes away your power and plants doubt about your expertise.

Recognizing trigger phrases as a listener helps you manage your reactions and stay composed during difficult conversations. By identifying these phrases and acknowledging their impact, you can remain calm and approach the dialogue with empathy rather than defensiveness. The biggest loss, though, is when one phrase doesn't leave your brain, and you don't hear anything after that phrase. Go ahead, admit it. You couldn't stop thinking about the absurdity of what was said and applied the same judgment to everything that was said afterward, even though you have no idea what was said.

CRITICAL CONVERSATIONS

Critical conversations, whether in the workplace or in personal relationships, require clear, direct, and respectful communication. As a speaker, it's important to articulate your points with precision while being open to feedback. In these moments, emotional intelligence and diplomacy are key to finding solutions. Look, you can't turn off emotions, but try to make sure they are not getting in the way of what you want to say.

For the listener, critical conversations demand patience and a willingness to fully understand the speaker's concerns before responding. Wait for it. Patience before responding. By actively listening, you help diffuse tension and create a space where both parties can collaborate on finding common ground.

INFLUENCE, COLLABORATE, AND NEGOTIATE

In any collaborative setting, the ability to influence others comes from how well you present your ideas and listen to responses. Negotiation requires a balance between assertiveness and openness, ensuring that all voices are heard and mutual benefits are achieved. Effective speakers know how to advocate for their ideas while remaining flexible.

Collaboration and negotiation thrive on the ability to listen to others' perspectives. By truly understanding the needs and priorities of others, you can more effectively influence outcomes and build partnerships that lead to successful negotiations. If you need clarity to fully understand what the speaker is communicating, then ask questions like: *"Help me understand what you are saying/offering or looking for...by clarifying."*

EMPATHY

Empathy involves speaking from a place of understanding what the listener may be going through emotionally. You communicate not only what needs to be done but also why it matters to the people involved, including the listener. As a leader, your words can inspire and guide your team, making empathy a powerful tool for building trust and loyalty.

People who listen empathetically create a more inclusive and supportive environment. By understanding the emotions and concerns of others, you demonstrate that their contributions are valued, which in turn strengthens the team and promotes open communication.

MANAGING UP

Okay, you are in charge. It doesn't mean you will be heard.

Managing up requires clear, concise communication when interacting with higher-ups and those who work for you. When you are in charge, it's essential to be solution-oriented, getting clear on priorities, and presenting ideas in a way that aligns with the goals of the business or project.

When managing up, listening to your supervisor's goals and expectations is just as important as speaking up. By understanding their vision and concerns, you can anticipate their needs and present solutions proactively, fostering a more productive working relationship. If you are uncertain of their goals and needs, or are receiving a confusing message, then ask them to repeat or clarify them.

Look, we all know the feeling of speaking up and wondering if anyone is really listening. As women, we've often been silenced or interrupted—our voices brushed aside. But here's the key to powerful communication: you can speak clearly and not be heard. Check in with your communication partner. Ask them, *"I'd like to hear your thoughts on what I shared."* Then pause. Wait for the answer.

DEVELOP YOUR COMMUNICATION SKILLS

1. **FIND YOUR AUTHENTIC VOICE:** So many of us have learned to adjust our tone or soften our language to avoid coming off as "too aggressive" or "too direct." But being authentic in how we communicate is key to gaining respect. Practice. Tape yourself. Hear what they are hearing. See what they are seeing as you walk through a conversation. Ask people for input. Trusted people.

   ACTIONABLE STEP: Next time you're in a meeting, resist the urge to downplay your ideas with trigger phrases like *"I'm just thinking..."* or *"This might be silly, but..."* Instead, speak directly and with confidence.

2. **LISTEN DEEPLY:** Communication isn't just about speaking. It's also

about listening—*active listening*—truly engaging with the person in front of you. When you listen with empathy, you're better able to respond thoughtfully, which elevates the entire conversation.

ACTIONABLE STEP: Practice active listening in your next conversation. Focus on what the other person is saying without planning your response ahead of time.

3. **OWN YOUR NARRATIVE:** How we talk about our achievements and experiences matters. Women often downplay their accomplishments or hesitate to advocate for themselves. Owning your story is essential to powerful communication and ultimate success.

ACTIONABLE STEP: Keep a journal of your daily or weekly

accomplishments. Women often forget or don't give themselves credit for achievements, saying, *"It wasn't me; it was the team,"* when without their leadership, the team would not have achieved anything. Practice articulating your successes, whether to yourself or in a small group of trusted friends. Get comfortable with self-advocacy.

OVERCOMING SOCIETAL AND HISTORICAL BARRIERS

Historically, women were expected to stay quiet, to be the "supporting cast" while men led the conversations. This cultural conditioning can make it difficult to fully step into our voices. To break free, we must rewrite the story. Your voice is valuable and deserves to be heard. When you speak with confidence and conviction, you give others permission to listen.

TIP: If you find yourself being interrupted in meetings, ask a coworker to jump in and say, *"Please let Joan finish. I want to hear her thoughts on that issue."* Agree ahead of a meeting to do this for each other. The same can be done when someone takes credit for a suggestion that you contributed only a few minutes earlier.

FROM THOSE WHO HAVE GONE BEFORE...

- **MELINDA GATES:** Melinda has used her platform to amplify the voices of women globally. Her communication style is both empathetic and powerful, blending facts with deeply personal stories that drive change.

- **BRENÉ BROWN:** Known for her work on vulnerability, Brené's communication style is deeply authentic. By speaking openly about her own challenges, she has built a global movement around courage and connection.

THOUGHTFUL QUESTIONS ON WHICH TO REFLECT

1. When do I feel most confident in my communication, and how can I recreate that?

2. What stories am I telling myself that limit how I use my voice?

3. How can I become a better listener to elevate my communication skills?

" *Effective communicators are, first and foremost, effective listeners. Only when you listen to your partners and understand their perspectives can you make informed choices about what to say or do.*"

— Judi Brownell, Professor of Organizational Communication, Cornell University

FUNDAMENTALS OF COMMUNICATION

- Effective communication is at the heart of building relationships, facilitating collaboration, achieving goals, and engaging and inspiring the people around you.

- The main ingredients of meaningful communication between two people are active listening, pausing, asking questions, and empathy.

- Creating a circle of influence to achieve your vision is built on how well you communicate.

- Preparation is everything. Every important conversation and meeting deserves an agenda of talking points to maximize value for all.

CHAPTER 7

RELATIONSHIPS

> "My relationships are
>
> the guides for my climb
>
> up to my vision."
>
> — Leslie Grossman

EVERYONE NEEDS THEIR OWN TEAM

Let's talk about something that can make a huge difference in your life: your support team. You might have heard the term "entourage," which I used in my last book. But ten years later, I have re-thought that term and have replaced it with "circle." What you need is a team or a circle of people that's got your back, like the friends in *Sex and the City*, or a women's basketball team supporting Caitlin Clark, the Indiana Fever, or not to show team preference, team members from the New York Liberty or Connecticut Sun. Caitlin is there for her team members, and they are there for her, both publicly and privately. When the draft took place, many of Caitlin's college teammates from the Iowa Hawkeyes attended, knowing they were not on the list to be drafted, and when she was, they cheered with authentic happiness. It's all about mutual support, cheering each other on, and lifting each other up. It's about helping your teammate get that goal and them passing you the ball so you can shoot and make the basket.

Imagine your support circle as a group of friends, business or professional relationships, and community connectors who are there for you through thick and thin. They're the ones who celebrate your victories and help you through challenges. Unlike a traditional network, which might just be a collection of business cards, a support circle is about deep, trusted relationships. These are the people you can count on for honest advice, support, and meaningful connections.

Think of it this way: Your support circle is like your own personal solar system. You're the sun, and those in your support circle are the planets. Each one brings something unique to the table, and together, you all shine brighter. It's a give-and-take relationship where everyone benefits. And, on their journey, they are the sun, and you are part of their solar system. Quid pro quo in the best of ways.

So, why do you need a support circle more than a network? A network might help you occasionally, but a support circle is there for the long haul. They're the ones who return your calls and emails, offer sincere communication, and provide consistent follow-up. It's a win-win situation where everyone is invested in each other's success, both professionally and personally.

Building a support circle takes effort, but it's worth it. It's not about competition; it's about collaboration. By working together, we can all achieve our goals. So, let's start building those relationships, supporting each other, and creating a powerful support circle that will help us all succeed.

FROM COMPETITION TO COLLABORATION

Many of us have been taught to think of our careers as solo journeys, where success means doing it all on our own. But the truth is, no one achieves greatness alone. The most successful people surround themselves with others who help them reach their goals.

Creating a circle of support means shifting our mindset from competition to collaboration. Instead of seeing others as rivals, we should see them as potential allies. By forming partnerships, we can achieve more together than we ever could alone. It's about building trusted relationships where everyone helps each other succeed.

THE POWER OF A CIRCLE OF SUPPORT

History is full of examples of powerful circles of support. Think about Madam C.J. Walker, America's first self-made woman millionaire, an independent hairdresser and manufacturer of hair care creams. An African American, she built a mail-order operation and trained hundreds of women around America to sell her products. Her support circle included her daughter, her husband, and the many women she trained to lead their own businesses and sell and demonstrate the products. As her business grew, so did her support circle, which included people like Booker T. Washington, Mary McLeod Bethune, and W.E.B. Du Bois. She expanded her reach and influence by becoming active in organizations and politics.

A modern-day example might include Taylor Swift. Her circle of support includes her family, friends in the industry, other artists who become collaborators, and Swifties—who support her in expanding the base of followers and responding to her offerings to them. She also shows her commitment to supporting those who support her. Her paying her truck drivers during the Era USA tour a bonus of $100,000 comes to mind. Or her events at her home when she is launching a new album, or during the tour, her choosing a spectator to present her famous hat to during a song, inviting her friends to parlay off her fans by performing a song on her stage.

AVENUES FOR FINDING YOUR CIRCLE OF SUPPORT

Successful humans know that some of the most important work happens outside the office. Attend conferences, join associations, volunteer for causes you care about, and make meaningful connections. These face-to-face interactions build strong relationships that form the foundation of a powerful support team. Give and ask. Both are critical components for building relationships.

BUILDING YOUR SUPPORT CIRCLE

So, how do you build your own circle of support? Start by reaching out and connecting with people who share your values and goals. Attend events, join groups, and volunteer your time. Be genuine in your interactions and look for opportunities to support others. Remember, it's a two-way street. The more you help others, the more they'll be willing to help you.

Think of your circle of support as your personal board of directors. These are the people you turn to for advice, guidance, and support. They offer a fresh perspective and can introduce you to new opportunities. Your circle is there to help you navigate your career and achieve your dreams.

Building a circle of support is essential for success. It's about creating a network of trusted relationships where everyone helps each other achieve their goals. By shifting our mindset from competition to collaboration, we can build a powerful support circle that will be there for us through all of life's challenges. So, start reaching out, building relationships, and creating your own circle today. Together, we can achieve amazing things.

No one succeeds alone. The relationships we build—in business and in life—are critical to our growth. But building meaningful relationships takes intention, trust, and authenticity, especially for women who have often been sidelined from critical networks.

HOW TO BUILD STRONG RELATIONSHIPS

1. **BE INTENTIONAL:** Building relationships isn't about networking in the traditional sense; it's about creating meaningful connections. Think quality over quantity.

ACTIONABLE STEP: Identify three to five key relationships you want to cultivate this year—whether they are mentors, peers, or potential collaborators. Reach out to them regularly with no agenda other than to learn about them, their visions and goals, and to build connections.

2. **GIVE AS MUCH AS YOU TAKE:** Relationships thrive on reciprocity. Offer support, advice, or mentorship without expecting anything in return. This builds trust and long-term value.

ACTIONABLE STEP: Consider how you can support the people in your network right now, without expecting immediate returns.

3. **SEEK DIVERSE CONNECTIONS:** Don't limit yourself to people who are just like you. The more diverse your network, the more opportunities you create to learn and grow.

ACTIONABLE STEP: Step outside your usual circles—attend an event or reach out to someone in a different field or industry.

OVERCOMING SOCIETAL AND HISTORICAL BARRIERS

Historically, professional networks have been dominated by men, often excluding women from key decision-making circles. But we are seeing a shift. Women are building their own networks and circles, supporting one another in unprecedented ways. To overcome this historical exclusion, we must continue to create and participate in spaces where women lift each other up.

FROM THOSE WHO HAVE GONE BEFORE...

- Arianna Huffington: Founder of The Huffington Post and Thrive Global, Arianna has always emphasized the importance of relationships in building her career, especially the role of mentorship and women supporting women.

- Whitney Wolfe Herd: The founder of Bumble built a business centered on connection and community, creating a space where women have the power to initiate conversations.

FOR REFLECTION...

1. What relationships in my life feel most supportive, and how can I deepen them?

2. How am I showing up for others in my network, and what more can I give?

3. How can I broaden my network to include voices and perspectives different from my own?

" *True leadership is when you build bridges, not walls, to foster strong relationships.*"

— Sheryl Sandberg, former COO of Facebook and author

FUNDAMENTALS OF RELATIONSHIPS

- No one is successful without supportive relationships.

- Collaborating and giving to others so they can succeed is at the heart of building trusted relationships.

- Relationships are a two-way street— with each person caring and contributing to the other. Be there for your circle. But don't forget to ask for introductions or a new way of thinking that would potentially benefit you.

- Conversations with each person listening actively to the other are the starting point of a potential relationship.

 CHAPTER 8
MINDSET

> "I know that when I have
> a clear, positive mindset,
> every single thing I do in a
> day is my best effort."
>
> —Leslie Grossman

Learning never stops. Research has proven that the process for living your vision and growing your career or business is within your reach, as long as you continue learning. Learning comes from many sources, with education being only one of them. We learn from conversations, discussions, experiences, curiosity, reading, relationships, and multiple sources. Let's start by giving up on believing we must always be "right."

Our mindset can address imposter syndrome and the inner critic, which many of us deal with. The techniques to break through self-limiting beliefs are part of the wealth of content in all the programs I lead.

Your mindset is the lens through which you view the world, and it can either propel you toward your goals or hold you back. For women, mindset is especially crucial because we are often battling against societal narratives about what we can or can't achieve.

HOW TO DEVELOP A GROWTH MINDSET

1. **CHALLENGE YOUR INNER CRITIC:** We all have that voice in our heads that tells us we're not good enough, or that we're impostors. The key to shifting your mindset is recognizing that voice for what it is: it is the voice of fear, not the truth.

   ACTIONABLE STEP: The next time your inner critic shows up, write down what it's telling you. Then, challenge it. Ask yourself, "Is this true, or is this fear talking?"

2. **EMBRACE FAILURE AS LEARNING:** Too often, women are socialized to fear failure, but failure is part of growth. Reframing setbacks as learning opportunities is key to developing a resilient mindset.

ACTIONABLE STEP: Keep a "failure journal." Each week, write down something that didn't go as planned and reflect on what you learned from it.

3. **FOCUS ON PROGRESS, NOT PERFECTION:** Perfectionism is often the enemy of progress. Give yourself permission to take imperfect action, knowing that growth happens in the process.

ACTIONABLE STEP: Set small, incremental goals and celebrate your progress, even if it's imperfect.

OVERCOMING SOCIETAL AND HISTORICAL BARRIERS

Women have historically been held to higher standards of perfection in the workplace, expected to prove their worth at every turn. Shifting your mindset away from these external pressures and toward self-defined success is critical.

FROM THOSE WHO HAVE GONE BEFORE...

- Jessica Herrin: Founder of Stella & Dot, Jessica has often spoken about the importance of a growth mindset and how embracing failure helped her build a multi-million-dollar business.

- Sophia Amoruso: Founder of Nasty Gal and author of #GIRLBOSS, Sophia built her brand by embracing risk and learning from her mistakes, emphasizing the power of a growth mindset in achieving success.

FOR REFLECTION...

1. What limiting beliefs are holding me back from achieving my vision?

2. How can I reframe my relationship with failure?

3. What steps can I take to challenge my inner critic and adopt a growth mindset?

" *Your mindset can propel you toward success or hold you back from achieving your dreams.*"

— Arianna Huffington, Founder of The Huffington Post and Thrive Global

FUNDAMENTALS OF MINDSET

▪ Mindset is created when your feelings impact your brain in either a positive or negative way, resulting in putting your own interpretation on what something means.

▪ Your beliefs become your thoughts. They can either wreck your judgment of yourself and others or create amazing opportunities that open doors for success and happiness. The choice is yours to make.

- You have the power to change your own mindset and open the door to opportunities, learning, growth, and change.

- A growth mindset enables you to embrace challenges, learn from failure, be eager to learn, accept change, and be persistent on the journey to your vision.

CHAPTER 9
COURAGE

"Courage doesn't always
involve physical danger.
Maybe we think of it that
way because society hasn't
wanted to acknowledge
that courage is needed
every time you step
out of the safety of
what you know."

— Leslie Grossman

Nelson Mandela said he learned that courage was not the absence of fear, but the triumph over it. It is natural to sometimes feel fearful when we move into new territory. That's when we need to dig into our bag of tricks and pull out those that move us forward beyond the fear. For instance, when we find ourselves fearful about what could go wrong, it's time to create a brain shift and focus on what could go right. Our minds are powerful. Most of us can learn to overcome the fear and focus on achieving the goal and our vision. Get comfortable with being uncomfortable. It's a positive sign to feel uncomfortable and to go do it anyway.

Courage isn't the absence of fear—it's taking action despite it. For women, especially, courage often means stepping into spaces where we haven't been welcomed, speaking up when it's easier to stay silent, or pursuing goals that others might deem impossible.

HOW TO CULTIVATE COURAGE

1. **TAKE SMALL STEPS OUTSIDE YOUR COMFORT ZONE:** Courage isn't about grand gestures; it's about small, consistent acts of bravery.

   ACTIONABLE STEP: Identify one thing you've been avoiding because it feels intimidating. Break it down into smaller steps, and commit to tackling just one this week.

2. **OWN YOUR FEAR:** The most courageous people aren't fearless— they simply acknowledge their fear and move forward anyway.

   ACTIONABLE STEP: The next time fear shows up, name it. Write down exactly what you're afraid of, and then ask yourself: "What's the worst that could happen?" Often, you'll realize the fear is manageable.

3. **SEEK OUT DISCOMFORT:** Growth doesn't happen in the comfort zone. The more you put yourself in situations that stretch you, the more your courage muscles grow.

   ACTIONABLE STEP: Make a list of situations that make you uncomfortable but could lead to growth. Start with the least intimidating one and make a plan to face it head-on.

OVERCOMING SOCIETAL AND HISTORICAL BARRIERS

Historically, women have been discouraged from taking risks. Society has often told us to be cautious, to play it safe, and to avoid stepping outside the lines. But times are changing, and we are rewriting the script. The courage to take risks and stand out is not only possible but necessary for us to break through barriers and create the future we envision.

THOSE WHO HAVE GONE BEFORE...

- **RUTH BADER GINSBURG:** RBG's career was a testament to courage. From fighting for women's rights in a male-dominated legal field to overcoming personal and professional obstacles, she consistently stood up for what she believed in, despite the risks.

- **SARA BLAKELY:** The SPANX founder started her company with a courageous leap, investing her life savings into an idea that many dismissed. Her journey is a powerful reminder of the importance of taking risks and believing in yourself.

FOR REFLECTION...

1. Where in my life have I been playing it safe, and how can I embrace more courage?

2. What would I pursue if I weren't afraid of failure or judgment?

3. How can I practice small acts of courage daily to build my resilience?

" *Courage is about doing what you're afraid to do. There can be no courage unless you're scared.*"

— Carly Fiorina, Former CEO of Hewlett-Packard and Author

FUNDAMENTALS OF COURAGE

- Courage is doing what needs to be done, taking action, even when you are fearful or uncertain of the outcome.

- When you navigate through uncertainty and do it knowing that it is the right thing to do, you are being courageous.

- Speaking up on your own behalf or for others can be an act of courage.

▪ Taking bold steps, especially when you are uncomfortable, is personal courage. Get comfortable with being uncomfortable!

CHAPTER 10
CONFIDENCE

> "Confidence comes from
> knowing you did every single
> thing you could before you
> arrived to present your best self
> and most authentic message."
>
> — Leslie Grossman

We feel confident as an outcome of embracing six of the Seven Leadership Tenets: Vision, Communication, Presence, Mindset, Relationships, and Courage.

When you incorporate them into your life, confidence comes with ease. You know where you are going. You are in motion to reach your vision through conversations with your many trusted relationships. You are not afraid to fail because you are clear that you are learning from each experience and even from your mistakes. You carry yourself with clarity, warmth, and understanding of others as well as yourself, and so you are perceived as a leader. You feel confident because you believe that most things happen for a reason to be revealed sometime in the future.

Just as we are putting this book to bed, the debate between Kamala Harris and Donald Trump took place on a world-wide stage, with the 2024 presidential election on the line. Just two short months before, Joe Biden's disappointing debate performance ended with him withdrawing from the race.

Pundits and those in Harris' inner circle said this was the night that could make or break her. Harris strode across the stage and intercepted DJT as he arrived at his podium, thrust out her hand, and said, "Kamala Harris. Good debate." He shook her hand and mumbled, "Nice meeting you," or something close to that. It was the last time he looked at her. She never stopped looking at him. Her confidence, which quite possibly could have been more stage than heartfelt, sent her to a debate that was seeped with her confidence in presentation and fact. But she earned the right to be on that stage.

CONFIDENCE SKILL BUILDING

COMPETENCY:

Yes, it's a skill. Invest time in developing it. Confidence grows from competence, so it starts with continuous learning in your area of expertise to build a solid foundation.

Think of the most confident people you know; both public personas and private people in your sphere of influence. Whatever their expertise, they know their stuff.

OWN THE WIN:

Acknowledge your achievements, no matter how small. Regularly recognizing progress boosts self-confidence. Don't be afraid to share them. With the right people. With those that will appreciate and be happy for you. You know who those individuals are. Keep and read your Daily Accomplishment Journal before a challenging meeting or event. Remind yourself of what you have done well. How much we forget!

STEP OUTSIDE YOUR COMFORT ZONE:

Consistently take on challenges that stretch your capabilities. Confidence is built from new wins outside our zone of comfort. Okay, you actually did something which you never thought you could do!

You will walk confidently in that arena. The more you face fear and uncertainty, the more resilient your confidence becomes.

POSITIVE SELF-TALK:

This is the hard one. The voice in our heads, which we think is always honest, is not. That voice has a job: to protect you in the future from pain in your past. It will sense danger when there might not be any. It will make you more nervous than you should be if you are pitching a great presentation for a potential new client. It doesn't want you to be disappointed. That negative Nellie doesn't get to be in your head.

Replace negative self-talk with affirmations. Develop a habit of talking to yourself as you would to a friend—supportive and uplifting. Sure-footed and, well, confident.

SEEK FEEDBACK AND IMPROVE:

Confidence isn't about perfection, but progress. Constructive feedback, from the right people, helps you identify areas of improvement and shows you're committed to growth. But you know what else it does? It reinforces how good you are at what you are attempting to do. Ask people to give you examples—if you need them—of why they think you are able to do what you are attempting to do.

BODY LANGUAGE:

Stand tall, make eye contact, and use open gestures. Your physical posture can impact how confident you feel and how others perceive you. Wear that outfit you know is your best look. Take the time to make sure you have the shoes, and the accessories that put you forward visually in your best light.

MINDFULNESS:

Practice mindfulness to stay grounded. Confidence grows when you can focus on the present without being overwhelmed by self-doubt or external pressures.

SET ACHIEVABLE GOALS:

Break larger goals into smaller, manageable tasks. Completing each step builds momentum and fosters confidence as you see your progress.

LEARN TO SAY NO:

Saying "no" is a powerful assertion of boundaries, and it shows confidence in your priorities and abilities. Saying no is a confidence builder that you might doubt, but perhaps that is because you never say it.

SURROUND YOURSELF WITH SUPPORTIVE PEOPLE:

Build a network of mentors and colleagues who believe in you. Their support can reinforce your confidence when you face

challenges. But in addition,
make sure they are confident in
themselves, and remind them of why
they have the right to be confident.

CREATE YOUR OWN AFFIRMATIONS:

Write and recite your very own
empowering statements, for
example: I am growing more and
more confident with each passing
day. I hope that never stops. And,
I assess my confidence level now
and again to make sure I am on
the right track.

MUSIC MAKING CONFIDENCE:

Create a confidence playlist. Play
it before you leave in the morning,
while you are driving to the meeting
or just before the conversation.
Choose the songs that remind you
how powerful you are...even when
you believe you are not.

CHAPTER 11

PAY IT FORWARD

I want to end with the most important thing. No matter what your vision, no matter how big (or small) your success, the opportunity to truly make a difference lies in the extent of your desire to pay it forward.

The women mentioned in this book? All of them paid or are paying it forward. Some more than others.

A critical part of one's success and happiness is to activate your "pay it forward" philosophy. This generosity should extend towards people in your circle, family, friends, and even strangers you happen to meet. You can activate your pay it forward philosophy through spontaneous acts of kindness, as well as more planned efforts to do good for others. Or most importantly, by sharing what you've learned to get where you are now, or where you are going. The lessons, the nuggets others gave you— those are what we all need to get from each other to be our best selves.

Just as you seek out mentors, offer to mentor someone who needs your experience to help them move forward in their career or improve at their job or small business. Or bring together a group of people who would benefit from knowing each other and encourage them to support each other with you leading the group. Offer to share your expertise on a given topic without any expectation of getting business from it.

Work with high school students at a low-income school, providing job or career advice. Take students on a school trip to meet business owners in their area to hear how they started and how they addressed their challenges, or organize an internship program. Think about how you can help your community as part of an organized association, or by starting your own. Doing good will not only kick in the serotonin, but it will also help you realize just how much you have to give to help others, even when your own confidence could use a boost. Paying it forward can shift the energy in the universe. Suddenly, you feel optimistic, and your business, career, or sales volume starts taking an upward turn.

When we look for opportunities to give back to someone with no expectation of any reward, we begin to see the entire world population as part of our circle. The world becomes a network of people making a difference in the lives of whomever they encounter—for the common good. When we all join together in this effort, not only will we lead the lives we want, but so will everyone around us, making the world a better place for everyone. Idealistic? Yes indeed.

As we connect to each other, we create several circles of connections. Each of our circles can interconnect with another circle of people. As this continues, an exciting discovery emerges: we are all connected. Together, we have formed a worldwide circle of mutual support. I like how that looks. I like how that feels. Do you? I believe the serotonin is kicking in.

I hope to hear from you about your journey and the lessons you've learned along the way. Perhaps I can feature your success in moving towards or reaching your vision in my next book.

To become part of my Circle and receive the Talking Circle Newsletter, visit my website at www.LeslieGrossmanVision.com and join my circles of collaboration. And, connect with me on LinkedIn.

ACKNOWLEDGEMENTS

In my book *Link Out: How to Turn Your Network into a Chain of Lasting Connections* published in 2013, I shared four pages of acknowledgements and gratitude to the many people who impacted my personal life and professional journey over many years. I again thank all of you mentioned in the *Link Out* acknowledgements pages. Here we are eleven years later, on the other side of a global pandemic, and I have many more to thank. The world has changed, and so have the challenges and the opportunities. My parents, who shaped my worldview, have left this planet but remain present through all they taught me. Thank you to my husband, Richard Abrams, of 50 years, my children, Josh and Sari, and my beautiful grandchildren, Mason, Skylar, Maya, and Ezra—all of whom keep me focused on the role that women play in impacting our future generations.

I learned how success and fulfillment begin with a personal vision of the future from my executive coach Tony Smith of VSA Consulting. His impact on me led me to become an executive coach, which was the first step in a new journey and a new vision that would impact girls, women, and their futures. Thank you to Vistage International for the opportunity to hone my skills as a coach and facilitator, and to learn first-hand the differences in how men and women lead their businesses and think. It was Lily Tang and Pamela Carlton who recruited me as a senior researcher for The Everest Project, where I learned about the strengths and qualities of women leading transformational change and innovation that has a profound impact on company culture. I owe deep gratitude to Ina Gjikondi, Director, Executive Education & Coaching at The George Washington University, who opened the door for me to create and teach the first Executive Women's Leadership Program for the university, now in its 9th year, where we impact both women's success and the organizations fortunate enough to have them as leaders. Thank you to all the women who have participated in the program, as well as my private clients, for all I have learned from you as well.

I conclude my acknowledgements with my most profound thank you to Christine Merser, strategist, writer, and founder of Blue2 Media. Christine and I reconnected after 20 years during the pandemic. Since then, she has served as my peer mentor, creative director, editor, podcast co-host, and a motivating force as I explore the path to achieving my own vision. It was Christine who advised me it was time to update *Link Out* in this new book *Start with Vision*, and direct it to my most important audience—women—and feature my new ideology—the 7 Tenets of Leadership—which is the foundation of all the work I do today. I will be eternally grateful.